CP/494

For Alan, Emma, Wilf and Ted, with love x – C.J–I.
For Jemima, with love – S.B.

The yoga breathing exercises and poses in
this book are great for children of all ages –
and grown-ups too! They can help bring a
sense of calm, boost energy levels or mood, or
just add a quiet, creative element to everyday
play. This book has been checked by a
qualified yoga instructor but was not written
as a set of instructions. It was designed for you
to enjoy with your child. Please don't leave
children to try poses unsupervised.

First published in Great Britain 2020 by Red Shed,
an imprint of Egmont UK Limited
2 Minster Court, 10th Floor, London EC3R 7BB

www.egmont.co.uk

Text copyright © Egmont UK Ltd 2020
Written by Susie Brooks
Consultancy by Emily Sharratt

Illustrations copyright © Cally Johnson-Isaacs 2020
Egmont UK Ltd and the illustrator have asserted their moral rights.

ISBN 978 1 4052 9614 4

A CIP catalogue record for this title is available from the British Library.

I Breathe

Susie Brooks Cally Johnson-Isaacs

Would you like to discover your own
SECRET SPECIAL POWERS?
All you really need to do is BREATHE!

With yoga, every breath can
take you on an adventure . . .

To the forest like a
STRONG, wise tree . . .

Through the jungle like
a BRAVE lion . . .

Up into the sky like an aeroplane soaring FREE! WHEEEEEEE!

Yoga can calm you down, cheer you up and make you feel READY FOR ANYTHING!

Lulu feels BRAVE, like a fearless lion.
She's not scared to climb up high!

Lulu takes a deep breath, sticks out her tongue,
then breathes out with a loud, proud ROAR . . .

Imagine you're a roaring LION too!

Feel brave enough
to try something new!

Becky and Ben feel READY, like buzzy bees.
There's lots to do, but they're still calm.

They shut their eyes and ears,
and gently close their mouths . . .
then they breathe out through their lips with a HUM.

Pretend you are a BEE, fluster-free!

Can you stay calm even when you're busy?

Daisy feels HAPPY, like a playful dog.
She's wide awake and having fun!

She stretches her legs and lifts her bottom high.

Dora lifts up one leg . . .

Dan waggles his tail!

Can you play at being a waggy-tailed DOG?

What makes you feel happy?

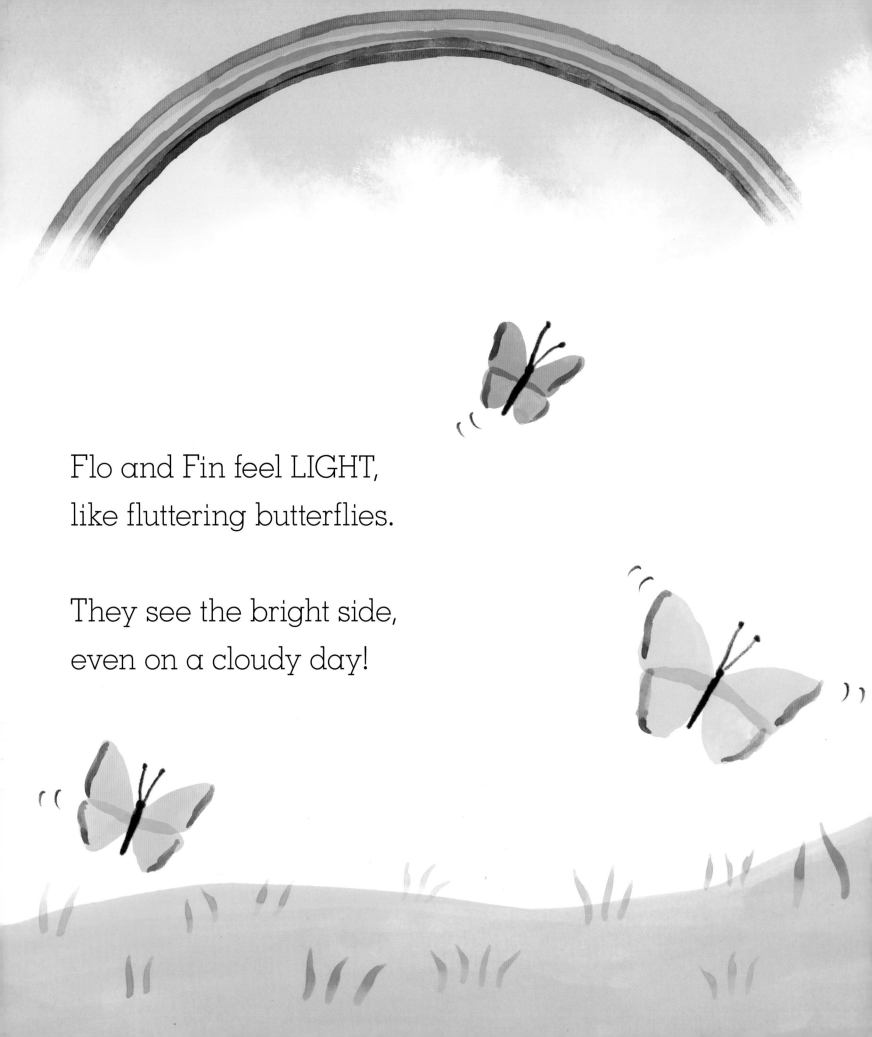

Flo and Fin feel LIGHT,
like fluttering butterflies.

They see the bright side,
even on a cloudy day!

They touch their feet together and gently flap their knees . . .

Imagine you are a colourful BUTTERFLY.

Feel light enough to fly away!

Billy feels RELAXED, like a floppy teddy bear.
He's daydreaming about all his favourite things!

With every deep breath,
   his belly lifts and lowers.

His teddy goes up . . .
   then down!

Try resting like a peaceful TEDDY BEAR.

What will you daydream about?

Tess and Tom feel STRONG,
like old, wise trees.

Their worries have blown
away with the breeze.

Tess's roots hold her steady
on the ground.

Tom reaches out his branches as he sways.

Imagine you are a mighty old TREE.

Feel strong and patient, even when you wobble.

Harry feels CHEERFUL, as if
a balloon is floating in his chest.
There's nothing weighing him down!

One long, deep breath in . . . then he gently puffs.

PHWV

Imagine you are a BALLOON floating in the sky.

WWWWWW.

How high will you fly and what will you see?

Mo feels CALM, like a sleepy mouse.
He's safe in his own quiet world.

He curls his body forwards and stays very still, breathing slowly.

Imagine you're the tiniest, quietest MOUSE . . .

Can you stay as still as can be without making a sound?

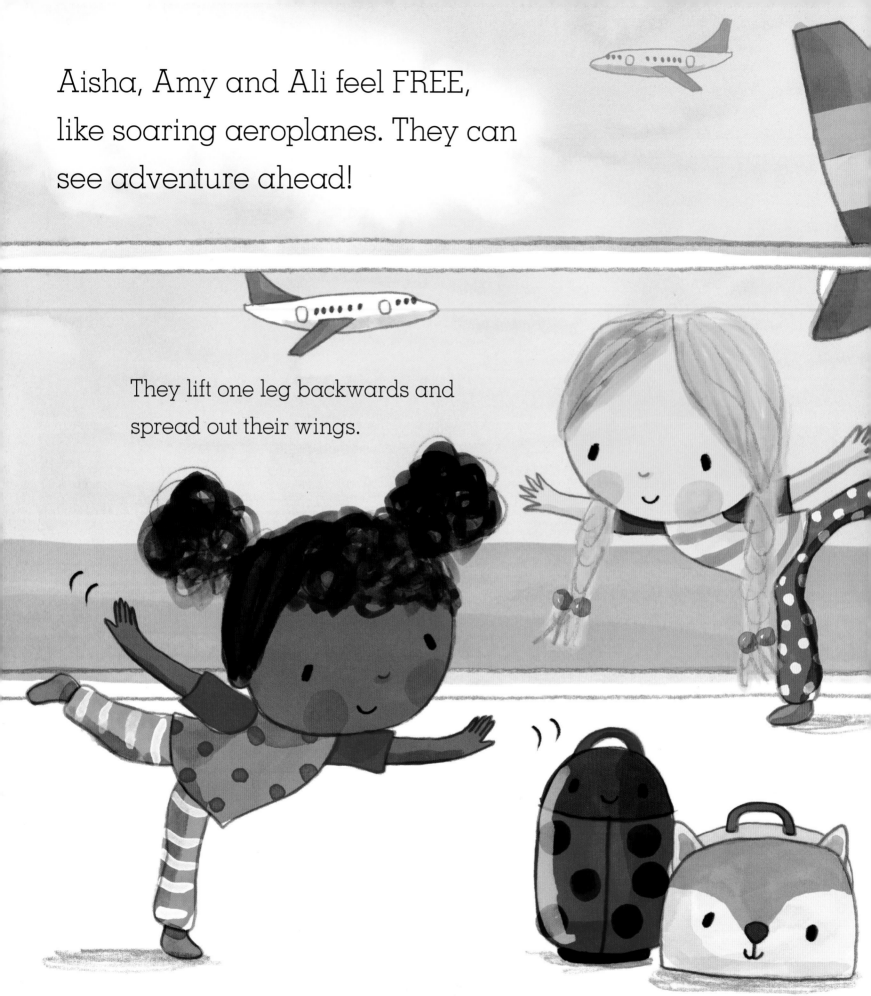

Aisha, Amy and Ali feel FREE, like soaring aeroplanes. They can see adventure ahead!

They lift one leg backwards and spread out their wings.

Ali leans his body forwards . . . WHEEEE!

Can you play at being an AEROPLANE, flying free?

Imagine the places you'll explore!

Alice feels ALERT, like a bouncy bunny.
All her tiredness has HOPPED away!

She takes three short sniffs . . .
then breathes out slowly.

Can you pretend to be a bouncy BUNNY?
Feel full of energy and ready to play!

You can use your yoga BREATHING POWER
whenever you need it.

If you're worried, relax like a TEDDY BEAR!

Fill your belly with soothing air.

When you're busy or flustered, be a BEE.

HUMMMMMM . . . That's better!

Blow away any sadness with a bright BALLOON.

PHWWWWWWW!

Sniffing like a BUNNY can help when you're feeling tired.

Don't be scared or shy – remember your

LION'S ROAR!